MW01121700

ENDANGERED!

SHARKS

Marc Tyler Nobleman

mc Marshall Cavendish
Benchmark
New York

Marshall Cavendish Benchmark
99 White Plains Road
Tarrytown, New York 10591
www.marshallcavendish.us

All Web sites were available and accurate when this book was sent to press.

Editor: Karen Ang
Publisher: Michelle Bisson
Art Director: Anahid Hamparian
Series Designer: Elynn Cohen
Cover Design by Kay Petronio

Front cover: A great white shark
Title page: A spined pygmy shark
Back cover: A grey nurse shark (top); a whale shark (bottom)
Photo research by Pamela Mitsakos
Front cover: Peter Verhoog / Minden Pictures

The photographs in this book are used by permission and through the courtesy of:
Minden Pictures: Mike Parry, 7; Flip Nicklin, 13; Alby Ziebell, 16; Alan James, 20; Tui de Roy, 36. Alamy:
DLILLC, 4; Redmond Durrell, 8; Marck Conlin / VWPICS, 9; Reinhard Dirscherl, 11; Ethan Daniels, 14;
Jeff Rotman, 1, 17, 18; Michael Patrick O'Neill, 19; Arco Images / Vnoucek, F., 22; Andre Seale, 27;
ArteSub, 42; Chris Gomersall, 43 (top); blickwinkel/Koenig, 28; Brandon Cole Marine Photography, 31.
Corbis: Jeffrey L. Rotman, 34; Bettmann, 37. SeaPics.com: 43 (bottom). Photo Researchers: Eye of Science, 26.
Peter Arnold: Jonathan Bird, 21, 24; Jeffrey L. Rotman, 30. Getty: Steve Winter, 32; Norbert Wu, 35;
Brian J. Skerry, 39; AFP, 40. Shutterstock: Keir Davis, back cover (top); Alexey Stiop, back cover (bottom).

Printed in China
1 2 3 4 5 6

Contents

1

Predators Become Prey

In silence, a fish the size of a large couch glides through the dark saltwater. Gradually, its triangle-shaped fin slices above the surface. The shark senses the humans before they realize it is coming. Suddenly there is thrashing. Blood swirls through the water. On the open sea, a life is lost.

The sight of a shark fin moving along the water's surface often makes people think of scary man-eating sharks. But in reality, the shark beneath is doing what it does naturally—swimming through water in search of food.

Is it a person or the shark? Because of the way sharks have been portrayed in scary movies and news stories, many people would assume that the shark attacked a person. However, humans kill many more sharks than the other way around. Sharks may be big, but boats are bigger. They may have sharp sets of teeth, but those teeth are no match for a harpoon, a hook, or even a net.

The twentieth century marked a tragic turning point for sharks. For millions of years, sharks have been the top **predator** in the ocean. They still are. Except for killer whales and other sharks, no marine animals hunt sharks. (Either they are not big enough or they do not eat meat.) However, now sharks are threatened by the top predator on land—humans.

Relying only on our bodies, we humans stand little chance against large carnivores such as lions or bears on land or sharks in the seas and oceans. Yet we have an advantage that these predators do not—a brain capable of developing technology. This technology makes up for what we lack in fangs, claws, or size. Fishermen use equipment that includes sonar for tracking marine animals, long

A great white shark is attracted to the bait at the end of this fishing line. Humans are the only animals capable of hunting down and killing great whites.

fishing lines with hundreds of hooks, wide nets, and machine-powered reels to catch sharks. Even more importantly, fisherman are able to use these tools on a boat, where they do not have to swim in the water with the sharks. Sharks are usually defenseless against these methods of capture.

KILLING MACHINES?

The idea of sharks as constant killing machines is largely inaccurate. Sharks can harm people, of course, but only a low percentage of them actually do. Scientists have classified more than three hundred **species**, or types, of sharks and continue to discover new ones. Fewer than

Strong jaws and sharp teeth are a necessity for most sharks.

Bull sharks are often dangerous to humans because these sharks tend to eat nearly any smaller animal they swim into. Some scientists believe that these sharks attack human swimmers out of curiosity or by accident.

thirty of those species have been known to injure humans. Of those, four species are responsible for most of the **unprovoked** attacks on humans—oceanic whitetip, bull, great white, and tiger sharks. All four of these species are vulnerable, threatened, or endangered, which means that their wild populations are decreasing and might soon disappear.

SHARK ATTACKS

In an average year, between 75 and 100 shark attacks are reported worldwide. Of those, usually fewer than 20 are fatal. In the United States, people report an average of 16 attacks a year. While even one shark-related injury or death is too many, these are low figures when compared to the total number of people who go in the water.

Yet all sharks, regardless of their size or historical behavior, are potentially dangerous. Like other animals, sharks may attack if threatened or confused. People can easily forget that every time a person and a shark meet unexpectedly, it is in the shark's territory. Some people believe that sharks are becoming more aggressive, or likely to attack, but that is not the reality. It only seems that shark attacks are on the rise because more people are going into the water than in the past.

Shark "attacks" are not always vicious as the word implies. In many instances, a shark mistakes a human for an animal it normally eats, such as a seal. Often, once

The largest shark—the whale shark—does not prey on humans. In fact, snorkelers and divers are often able to swim alongside these endangered giants.

the shark realizes that mistake, it leaves. It may have already taken a bite, but if help is nearby, the injured person often survives. Sharks may also bite to defend their territory.

However, considering the endangered state of sharks today, the term "shark attack" has the opposite meaning, too. Statistics show that sharks are usually victims, not

DID YOU KNOW?

Each of the following kills more people a year than sharks do: lightning, snakes, dogs, deer, elephants, pigs, bees, mosquitoes, falling coconuts, and even Christmas trees lights that electrocute people. At the seaside, people are more often injured by stepping on sharp seashells than by getting bitten by sharks.

villains. People worldwide kill between 30 and 100 million sharks each year. This has reduced the total shark population quite a lot—between 30 and 90 percent in some species. The World Conservation Union has more than two hundred types of sharks on its threatened and endangered species list. Scientists do not know how many sharks are in the oceans, but they can estimate that at least seventy-five shark species are on the verge of extinction, or disappearing forever.

In the last several decades, people have begun to protect sharks. Some countries have created laws to regulate shark fishing. Conservation groups are

Strung together by strong fishing lines, these dead sharks are dragged through the water by a fishing boat. Their fins, skins, teeth, and meat will be used for food, souvenirs, and other products.

running advertisements to educate the public about the cruelty of some fishing practices. Individuals are making a difference, too. For example, some people refuse to buy products made from sharks. Yet despite these actions and many others, sharks are still greatly at risk.

2

Life as a Shark

Sharks are fish. About 7 percent of all living fish species are sharks. Some sharks are as big as a bus and others are smaller than a banana. The largest known shark—the whale shark—is also the largest known fish. This endangered shark can grow to be up to 50 feet (15.2 meters) long. The second-largest fish is also a shark—the endangered basking shark.

A whale shark—along with some smaller fish—swims through the Indian Ocean. Some scientists think that these small fish stay close for protection from large predators and also to feed on the same food as the whale shark. A few of these smaller fish will even eat the parasites off of the whale shark's skin.

SHARK HABITATS

Sharks exist in oceans worldwide, particularly in warm regions. Some species live in cool to cold water. Most sharks are cold-blooded, which means that they get their heat from sources outside of their bodies, such as from the warm rays of the Sun. An average shark's body temperature is usually the same as the water around it.

Many different kind of sharks can be found living around coral reefs. The reefs attract a lot of fish, squid, and other sea creatures that the shark can eat. Destruction of coral reefs in some parts of the world has led to a decrease in certain shark species.

However, the body temperature of several species, including the great white, mako, porbeagle, and salmon sharks, can raise at least 15 degrees Fahrenheit (9.4 degrees Celsius) above the temperature of the surrounding water. This gives them the energy to swim faster, which enables them to catch prey more successfully.

Some sharks stay in one area. Others travel great distances, especially when their prey does. Certain types of sharks are more likely to venture close to shore while others remain near the sea floor, rarely seen by people.

The spined pygmy shark—which is usually less than a foot long—lives deep in the ocean and rarely comes into contact with humans. Some parts of these sharks actually glow in the dark.

Baby sharks, or pups, are born with the same features as adults—they are just smaller. A scientist holds a baby hammerhead shark that will grow up to look just like its parents.

THE LIFE CYCLE

Pups, or shark babies, are born in one of three ways. Some hatch from eggs outside of their mother. These sharks are known as oviparous. Viviparous sharks are born live, much like human babies are. Most, however, are ovoviviparous and hatch from eggs while the eggs are still inside their mother. Then those hatched sharks are born live. Most female sharks can have anywhere from one to seventy-five babies at time.

Some animals—such as frogs or butterflies—begin their lives in a form that is different from an adult's body. However, baby sharks resemble smaller versions of their parents. They just grow larger as they age and feed.

Shark parents do not care for their newborns, which are immediately able to feed on their own. Most sharks are solitary and live on their own. Some, however, travel in pairs or even in schools with many other sharks. Alone or in groups, male and female sharks do need to interact with each other in order to reproduce.

Scientists do not know for sure the life spans of most wild shark species. They estimate that most sharks can live up to twenty-five years. However, one type of shark—the spiny dogfish—may live for more than seventy years.

DIETS

Shark diets vary from species to species. For larger sharks, common prey include seals, sea lions, squid, turtles, and fish. These sharks seek out weaker or older animals because they are easier to overpower. Bottom-dwelling sharks, such as angel sharks, use

Most sharks do not chew their food. Instead, they swallow it in chunks.

their upper jaws to pick up crabs and clams. Their flat teeth then crush the food.

Though whale and basking sharks are the biggest shark species, they do not go after big prey. These big sharks do not have teeth. Instead they swim slowly with their massive mouths open, collecting large amounts of plankton and other small creatures. These organisms are filtered through the sharks' special gill structures.

Basking sharks are filter feeders. This means that they swim around with their big mouths open, sucking in water and small sea creatures.

Many sharks begin to feed at dusk and continue to hunt at night. Sharks frequently use surprise when hunting. Some sharks approach prey from below and rocket up to

A tiger shark is attracted to the chum inside this container. Fishermen, researchers, and shark-watchers use the chum to lure the sharks close.

grab it. Bottom-feeders hide on the seafloor and wait for prey to pass close enough to snatch. For faster sharks, pursuing prey is exhausting. Some do not need to feed

A great white leaps from the water with a seal in its powerful jaws. Unfortunately, these master predators are no match for humans and their technology.

every day. Sharks do not sleep in the way humans do, but they do have periods of rest.

All sharks are meat-eaters, but technically none are born man-eaters. Sharks do not target humans as food because humans are not a natural part of their environment. Also, sharks need fatty meat for energy. Compared to blubbery sea lions, for example, humans are hardly fatty enough to be desirable. That is why reports of "attacks" often describe a shark biting a person only once. The shark does not like what it tasted and essentially spits it out.

Wherever they live and whatever their prey, sharks are efficient hunters and eaters. Yet their skills do not help them avoid being hunted themselves. At times, their instincts may even put them in danger. Fishermen and shark hunters sometimes use chopped fish and other edible matter called **chum** to attract sharks to their boats, where the animals become easier targets. Studies have shown that some species are smarter than scientists previously thought, but few sharks seem to be smart enough to dodge human traps forever.

3

Shark Bodies

Most sharks are like living jets. The bodies of many species are designed to "fly" through the water with speed. Many sharks are rounded in the middle and then narrow to points at their snout (nose) and tail. This shape allows them to swim without being slowed down much by the water pressure around them. Shark species that move less have flatter bodies.

Though they may look odd, scalloped hammerhead sharks pose no threat to humans. Like other hammerheads, these sharks' eyes and nostrils are found on either end of their stalklike heads.

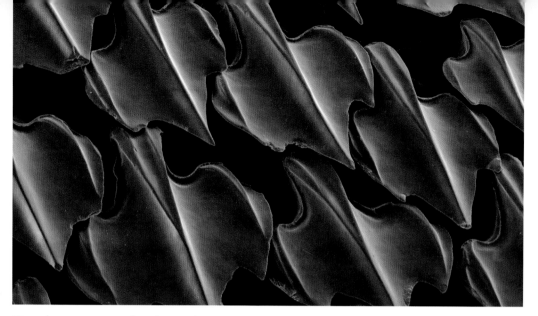

Teeth are not a shark's only weapon. If rubbed a certain way, the denticles on a shark's skin (shown here magnified more than seventy times) are sharp enough to injure other animals.

Sharks can be various shades of gray, brown, yellow, or blue. Some sharks have markings such as spots or stripes. Many sharks are camouflaged by countershading. Their tops are dark so they blend in with the ocean depths when viewed from above. Their bellies are light so they blend in with the lighter water near the surface when viewed from below.

Millions of tiny, tooth-like scales called denticles cover a shark's body. This rough skin feels like—and has been used as—sandpaper. Denticles do not grow bigger as the shark grows. Instead, the shark grows more denticles.

STRANGE SKELETONS

All sharks share certain traits that other fish do not have. Most fish—like many other animals, including humans—have skeletons made of bone. However, a shark skeleton is made of cartilage, not bone. Cartilage is a substance that is softer than bone but solid enough to be supportive. The flexible parts of your nose and ears are made of cartilage.

A shark's fins help it to balance and steer through the water. This sicklefin lemon shark is a species that is considered vulnerable, and may soon become threatened or endangered.

A shark has multiple fins—on the top and bottom of its body, along the sides, and at the end of the tail. These fins are framed by rods of cartilage. They are rigid and usually pointed. Fins help a shark move through the water. They also are a leading cause of endangerment for many shark species. Many shark species have been over-hunted for their fins, which are used in expensive soups.

JAWS

Shark mouths contain multiple rows of teeth. The front row is in active use and the other rows are like built-in backups. As front teeth wear down or fall out, teeth from

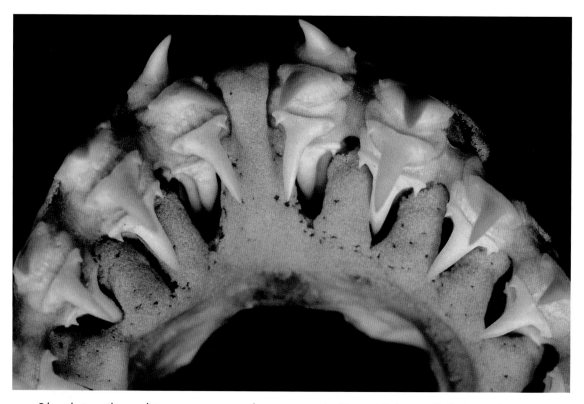

Shark teeth and jaws are popular souvenir items. Most of the teeth and jaws come from non-endangered sharks that were used for meat and other products. Sometimes, however, endangered species are used to make these products.

inner rows move forward to replace them. Typically, a shark has about five rows of teeth at a time and may go through 50,000 teeth in its lifetime. When combined with the strong force of its jaws, a shark's teeth can do serious damage to its prey.

SHARK SENSES

Sharks use their senses to detect prey and to observe what is going on in their environment. A shark's sense of smell is sensitive enough to pick up the scent of a large amount of blood that is a quarter of a mile away. Sharks have good vision and scientists believe they see in color. To protect their eyes, some species have eyelids called nictitating membranes while others are able to roll their eyes back into the sockets. Shark ears are inside their heads. Sharks are especially able to hear low frequency sounds that sick or injured animals give off.

Sharks can also sense other signals coming from other creatures in the water. All living animals give off small amounts of electricity. Sharks have electroreception,

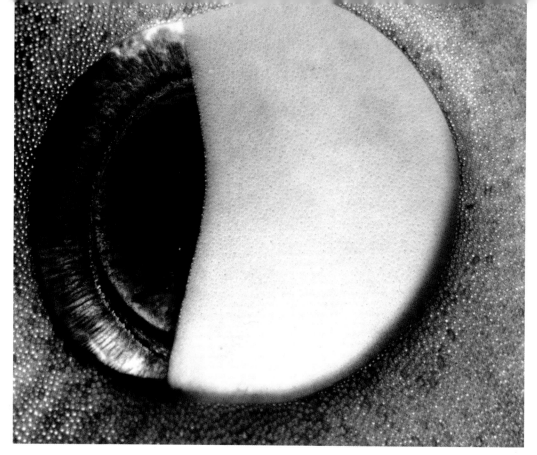

A shark uses its nictitating membrane to protects its eyes.

which is the ability to detect those signals at close range. They can also sense vibrations through lateral lines. These lines are a collection of cells that runs along the sides of a shark's body.

Shark bodies give them many advantages. Unfortunately, because humans see different types of advantages in shark bodies, many species have been fished or hunted to dangerously low levels.

All sharks have little cells called ampullae of Lorenzini (shown here as dark dots) on their snouts. These electroreceptors help them detect and send out small electrical signals.

4

Saving the Sharks

The fearsome reputation of sharks is not the main reason humans kill so many of them. Most of the people who kill sharks are commercial fishermen making their living. In some parts of the world, they have over-fished the oceans to satisfy the demand for seafood, but that has created a double problem. Fishermen are catching so many non-shark fish that they are depleting the overall fish population. That lessens the amount of food available

Shark fins cut from many different sharks dry in the sun. Shark fins are big business for many fishermen. In some places, a bowl of shark's fin soup can sell for $100.

for sharks. At the same time, with fewer fish to catch, fishermen go after sharks. In either case, sharks lose—and people do, too.

CATCHING SHARKS

Shark Parts

Fishermen catch sharks for multiple purposes. In countries including Mexico and certain African nations, shark meat is a major part of the diet. Throughout Asia, shark fin soup is a luxury. Shark fins sell for much higher prices than

A diver holds the dead body of a finless shark. Fishermen caught these sharks, cut off their fins, and then threw them back into the water. Without their fins, the sharks cannot move and eventually drown and die.

In a fishing village on the coast of Mexico, the hot sun dries the shark skins spread out on racks.

shark flesh. This has led to finning, which is a controversial practice in which fishermen cut off shark fins, then dump the rest of the animal back into the ocean. Without their fins, the sharks sink to the bottom where they will die.

Other parts of shark bodies become ingredients in a variety of products. Shark liver oil is mixed into cosmetics and creams. Some people believe that shark cartilage can ward off or even cure diseases, notably cancer, though studies have not shown that to be true. Shark skin is used to make leather shoes, belts, and bags. Shark teeth are sold as souvenirs.

A shark is caught up in a fishing net meant for other types of fish. In many countries, certain types of fishing nets have been outlawed because they trap too much bycatch.

Accidental Deaths

More than half of shark deaths caused by humans are accidental. Millions of sharks each year get stuck in fishing gear such as nets meant for tuna, shrimp, or other sea creatures. Unable to struggle free, the sharks die. This is called bycatch, and it is hugely wasteful because fishermen who would not get a good price for shark meat simply throw it away.

Hunting for Sport

Sometimes sharks are hunted for sport. Catching a large shark was a sign that a fisherman was strong and skilled. At one time, sharks were considered a worthless fish—dangerous nuisances at beaches and swimming "garbage cans" that

Shark fishing for sport has been around—and will continue to be around—for many years. In the past, many fishermen caught huge numbers of the same kind of shark, decreasing wild populations. These grey nurse sharks were caught off of the coast near Sydney, Australia.

Three common methods fishers use to catch sharks are placing a long line of hooks in the water, setting a large net wall underwater, and encircling sharks with a large net. The long lines can have up to 800 hooks and stretch out for ten miles. Unfortunately, these methods catch just about any kind of fish or marine mammal that travel that way—not just sharks. These methods are very productive, which means the fishermen can catch many fish, but there is no way to prevent the nets and hooks from catching endangered sharks—and other endangered marine life—whose numbers are already very low.

would eat anything. When shark hunters killed them, the public generally did not mind. It is true that sharks can be a threat along coasts, and many have been found with unusual items in their stomachs—including tires! However, we now know that sharks are important marine animals. Yet hunters continue to kill them because a shark still makes an impressive trophy, and often a good story, too. Many also use the excuse that they killed the shark before it went ahead and killed a person.

IN DANGER

Sharks are being killed faster than they can reproduce. Some species cannot begin to have babies until they are twenty years old, or even older. Many female sharks have only one or two pups every two years, unlike other fish which may have many hundreds more. These factors make it difficult for sharks to recover from over-fishing.

The oceans need sharks. They help preserve the balance of nature by preying on certain animals whose populations would otherwise grow too large. Overly large populations of certain types of fish in turn affects other fish populations and marine life.

CONSERVATION EFFORTS

Governments, organizations, and everyday citizens are working hard to improve the situation for sharks. People have urged officials to limit the amount of sharks that

Scientists catch and weigh wild shark pups before attaching special radio tags. These tags will help the scientists track wild shark populations. This kind of information can help determine if certain shark species are in danger and what can be done to help.

These protestors are showing their government officials that they care about the decreasing populations of the grey nurse shark. Whether it is collecting donations for wildlife protection or writing letters to government officials who make laws that affect animals, everyone can do something to help endangered species.

fishermen are allowed to catch. Some organizations sponsor a program in which people can pay to "adopt" a shark. The money is used to fund shark research and conservation efforts. Wildlife protection groups establish reserves, sections of the ocean where sharks can live and breed with no human interference.

For years, people around the world have condemned finning. They insist that the practice is cruel and should be illegal. Many countries—including the United States—have placed bans on finning. Unfortunately, these regulations are not always enforced.

At some beaches, large nets are set up underwater beyond the swimming area. They are intended to stop sharks and people from having any unplanned—and unpleasant—encounters. However, such nets have drawbacks. They are expensive and, like fishing nets, often lead to the deaths of animals that get snagged in them. Also, they cannot be used in water that is not calm. Researchers are developing an electronic barrier that would do the same job as the nets. It would send off electric signals that sharks find uncomfortable but not harmful. If this electric system works, then fewer accidental animal deaths may occur.

Anyone can help save sharks simply by not buying any shark products. If enough people do this, stores will stop carrying those products. That may send a message to companies that kill more sharks than necessary for human gain. It will show these companies that people would rather go without shark products than see sharks vanish from our oceans.

Sharks have lasted millions of years without human protection—but without human hunting, either. As a species, sharks were built for long-term survival. Yet to survive the new challenges they face in the modern world, they need human understanding more than ever.

SHARK SPECIES IN DANGER

The World Conservation Union (IUCN) has listed more than two hundred shark species as vulnerable, threatened, or endangered. That means that wild populations of these species could become extinct. Here is some information about some of these sharks.

SICKLEFIN LEMON SHARK

The sicklefin lemon shark lives close to shores in the tropical waters of the Pacific and Indian Oceans. It has been heavily fished. Some countries, including India, have already declared it extinct in their waters.

Sicklefin lemon shark

WHALE SHARK

The whale shark is a wide-ranging, slow-moving species. Found in tropical waters worldwide, its numbers have decreased due to heavy fishing for food. The Philippines placed it under protection in 1998 and Taiwan banned whale shark fishing as of 2008.

BASKING SHARK

Basking shark

The basking shark swims in colder waters. A gentle giant, it has been in demand for international trade, particularly for its fins. Scientists believe its population was not large to begin with, making over-fishing an even greater danger to the species. Some countries now legally protect the basking shark.

GREAT WHITE SHARK

The great white shark is found near coasts around the world. Due to its ferocious image, people who kill and sell parts of these sharks often charge—and receive—more money for them. Though some governments protect the great white shark, the laws are not easily enforced.

TOPE SHARK

The tope shark has been heavily hunted for its meat, oils, and fins. Australia and New Zealand have enacted fishing regulations, but the tope shark is unprotected in most other regions. If over-fishing of this species occurs, its wild populations will decrease.

Tope shark

GLOSSARY

bycatch—Unwanted marine animals that are accidentally caught with the animals that were supposed to be caught. For example, sharks and dolphins trapped in nets for small fish are considered bycatch.

cartilage—The soft, flexible substance that shark skeletons are made from.

chum—Ground-up fish and other edible matter put in the ocean to attract sharks.

cold-blooded—Describes animals whose body heat is determined by their environment. Fish are cold-blooded, while humans are warm-blooded.

conservation—The act of protecting nature, such as wildlife.

denticles—Toothlike scales that make up shark skin.

electroreception—The ability to detect weak electric signals. Sharks use the ampullae of Lorenzini on their heads to detect electricity.

extinction—The point when no more members of an animal species are living.

gill—An organ that helps fish such as sharks breathe.

nictitating membrane—A special lid that protects a shark's eyes.

predator—An animal that hunts other animals for food.

prey—An animal that is hunted.

pup—A baby shark.

regulate—To make sure rules are obeyed.

reserve—An area where wild animals live under human protection.

unprovoked—Describes an action that happens without warning or without reason. For example, a shark attack that happens to someone who is not interfering or bothering a shark is an unprovoked attack.

FIND OUT MORE

Books

Davies, Nicola. *Surprising Sharks*. Candlewick, Cambridge, Massachusetts, 2005.

Mattern, Joanne. *Sharks*. New York: Benchmark Books, 2002.

Savage, Stephen. *Access—Sharks*. New York: Kingfisher, 2007.

Spilsbury, Richard. *Great White Shark: In Danger of Extinction!* Chicago: Heinemann Library, 2004.

Web Sites

Clickable Shark
http://www.pbs.org/wgbh/nova/sharks/world/clickable.html

Oceana—Endangered Sharks
http://www.oceana.org/sharks

Shark Basics
http://www.flmnh.ufl.edu/fish/education/questions/Basics.html

Ten Cool Things You Didn't Know About Great White Sharks
http://www.nationalgeographic.org/ngkids/0206/shark_cage.html

WildAid's Shark Conservation Program
http://www.wildaid.org/index.asp?CID=72

ABOUT THE AUTHOR

Marc Tyler Nobleman has written more than sixty books for young people and one for adults. His titles include *Vocabulary Cartoon of the Day*, *What's the Difference?*, and *365 Adventures*. He also writes regularly for *Nickelodeon Magazine*.

INDEX

Pages numbers in **boldface** are illustrations.